The Lost Branch

Jackie Fischer

Outskirts Press, Inc.
http://www.outskirtspress.com

ISBN: 978-1-4787-6871-5

Library of Congress Control Number: 2017901330

Illustrated by: Marialuisa Paladino
Coordinator of Photos: Francesca Paladino

Outskirts Press and the "OP" logo are trademarks belonging to Outskirts Press, Inc.

PRINTED IN THE UNITED STATES OF AMERICA

By Jackie Fischer
Illustrated by: Marialuisa Paladino
Coordinator of Photos: Francesca Paladino

Author's Dedication

I dedicate this book to my late grandfather Charles (Carlo) Titone whose dream was always to be reunited with his lost brother, Gaspare Titone. It was his strength and persistence passed down through his family that enabled the family to be together once again. Although the family is separated by an ocean, technology allows us to communicate daily and keep the love and commitment to each other.

Author's Acknowledgement

I would like to give a special thank you to my cousin Annie who worked so hard on the extensive family tree. To my cousin, Anita, who provided us with some of the research. To my mom, Fran, also known as the movie star, who coordinated and supported the efforts of her cousins to have this remarkable reunion. My mom has been an inspiration my entire life to me and to many of her relatives and friends. To all who know my mom she is: an amazing mom, grandma, special education teacher, college professor and aunt, cousin, neighbor, cat lady and close friend. To my Dad who was one of a kind. It was because of him looking out for me from heaven that I had the courage to write this story. To my husband, Ira, who I love and cherish and to my son, Jonathan, who has shown me with determination, anything can be achieved!

To my family and new friends in Sicily, this book is for you! Our experiences, memories, chats and travels have brought us together and inspired the true story of our two families. Thank you from the bottom of my heart.

Illustrators Dedication to the Author

I met someone special; she has some years older than me,
But sometimes she can be a kid and that is funny, you will see
She is like a general who decides the rules,
But she is also like a doctor who takes care of you
She likes to play sports to relieve stress
And she can be a clown to make you laugh which she does best
She is full of energy with what everything we do
So it's hard to make plans because we don't know if it's going to last an hour or two
She puts her heart in her job and in her life and home
She loves her family whether in person or on the phone
She is a little crazy just like me,
This is why we agree!
I have spent with her a very short time
But it is almost like she has known me since I was nine
She lives far away,
but I always feel close to her in some way
she is a wonderful person, we spent beautiful moments together
and I hope that our friendship will last forever!
Having known her made me lucky
She is a great friend and cousin and her name is Jackie!

Table of Contents

Introduction

This story begins when…

Jackie's Grandfather Carlo arrived at Ellis Island with the clothes on his back and a suitcase. It was a very emotional journey to come to America. He was excited to live in New York but also very sad that his brother Gaspare was not able to come to America. He was sent back to return to their homeland of Sicily to live with an aunt and uncle.

In this poetic narrative there are two families separated by the sea but united by fate many years later. The Lost Branch describes the lives of two Italian families, one living in America and one in Sicily. Even though the branch was lost, the roots were still connected.

This heartwarming story enlightens the reader about Italian immigration in the early 1900's. It depicts how special cousin friendships, dreams and hopes develop, while taking you on a journey through Sicily, New York, Rome, Washington D. C and some other exciting adventures.

"General," "Giggles," "Muscles" and the "Movie Star" are cousins that connect in a special way. Though difficult to explain, their lives are completely different yet amazingly the same.

CHAPTER 1

Sicily to New York - The Long Journey

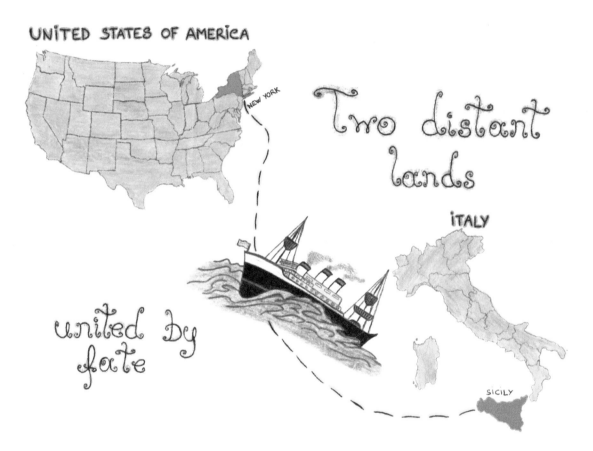

The times were tough during the day and night.
It was hard to get money to pay for the lights.

A family in Sicily was trying to get by,
They knew it was going to be hard but they had to try.

In 1914, there was a big ship departing that day
It was headed to New York City, it was a Friday.

The sea was scary, the waves were high,
The family of five had to take this ship, they could not fly.

Two boys and their sister, and their mom and dad,
Said goodbye to their homeland and were feeling very sad.

There were cries of sadness mixed with cries of despair,
From the young boys who had no place to sleep, not even
a chair.

The ship sailed a long 25 days and into the night,
These children were scared and truly experienced fright.

When they arrived in New York, Ellis Island, the hard
journey had come to an end.
A new chapter of life was about to begin for a family that
followed the trend.

Upon exiting the ship, medical exams were done.
The family had to be tested and that was no fun.

The immigration police were strict and mean.
They took the 12 year-old boy (Gaspare) away from his
father (Tommaso) and he let out a scream!

The mother (Anna) could not believe this to be true.
The police insisted the oldest son go back to Sicily, and the
ship's horn blew.

It was because of a concern with his left eye.
The immigration police took him away, and that's why!

Gaspare was going through this all alone.
He desperately wanted to be with his mom and dad in
their new American home.

He thought of his brother Carlo and how his life would be,
His family would be growing in the USA, and he could not
see.

A boy separated from his family across the sea.
What kind of life would he have? What would happen to his family tree?

An aunt and uncle cared for him when he got back.
It was really hard for him to stay on track.

This new family did their best,
But in the end, Gaspare knew they favored all the rest.

He never received one single letter from his family in the USA.
His new adopted family in Sicily threw them all away.

Young Gaspare pretended to look through a crystal ball.
He wished he knew what his American family was like, were they short or were they tall?

Did they wonder about him?
Did they know how to swim?

It was hard to imagine that he would never see,
The rest of his family on the family tree.

So he decided it was time to move on,
Leave this family that was not good to him and be gone.

CHAPTER 2

The Italian Family: Life in Sicily

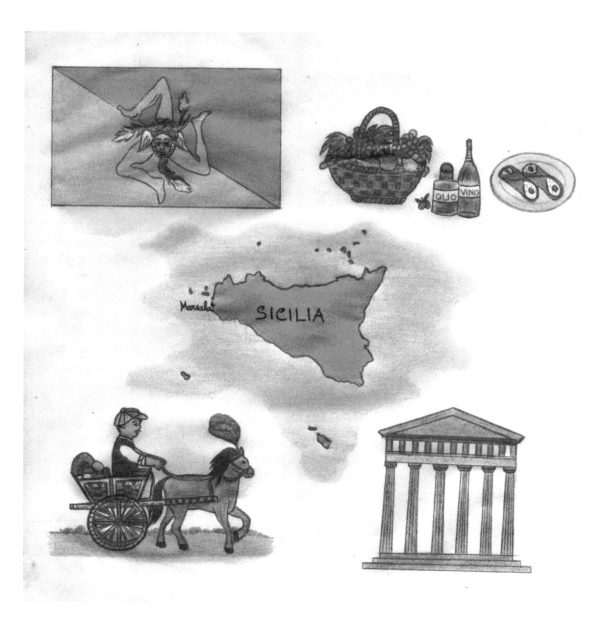

Gaspare's teenage years in Sicily were rough.
He missed his parents and siblings and that was very tough.

Gaspare went from job to job sometimes working a double.
Struggling to pay the bills and trying to staying out of trouble.

As a young man, he thought he could try again and see
To find and contact his American family.

There was no money and no hope.
The brothers were lost across the sea and had to cope.

He managed through the hard times as the years went by,
He met a girl named Giuseppa and they gave it a try.

Giuseppa was **bella** with her hair so long,
She loved music and enjoyed singing her favorite Italian song.

Wedding bells in a church near the sea,
The sound was echoing throughout Italy.

Love was what this young man had.
He was finally happy and glad.

He always thought of his parents, brother and sister in New York City
Wondering why they never kept in touch, it was a pity.

Gaspare always thought that his brother Carlo would be so proud of him.
He worked hard and it was tough to live in Italy without his kin.

There was barely enough food on the table for each meal
One time the thought crossed his mind, should I steal?

He knew right from wrong and would never do that.
He would provide for his family and even for their cat.

At 38 years old Gaspare was proud to have his own place
Giuseppa wanted to start a family and now they had their space.

Soon to follow, a son was born, Tommaso was his name.
With similar looks, they were like the same.

Five more children were born over the years- it was hard work but also fun
Two boys and four girls, new branches of a Sicilian family tree had begun.

**Gaspare with his
wife Giuseppa
With their first
son Tommaso**

Tommaso at age 26

CHAPTER 3

Tommaso – The Love of Family

Tommaso, Gaspare's oldest son,
The story of his family has now begun.

The City of Marsala was the place Tommaso called home.
Times were changing including the invention of the phone.

Life to Tommaso was to love and to care,
Every day he wished he would have a family to share.

As a teenager, he realized he had relatives in the USA,
But where, he wondered, would they let him come and stay?

How could I find them he said?
Would my aunts and uncles in America offer me a bed?

He would dream at night and wish upon a star,
That one day he would meet his American family that was so far.

But for now, Tommaso worked hard, hammering away,
He was building his house day by day.

Built with sweat, tears and love,
it was his **casa** and as he looked up, the birds flew above.

In that same year,
A special someone did appear.

It was fate at last,
That Maria came into his life to forget his past.

Tommaso and Maria Wedding

In Sicily, it was a tough life
For Tommaso and Maria, his lovely wife.

But in September of 1967, a baby **ragazza** came along,
it was a very happy day when she was born.

She was named after her grandmother, Giuseppa with
brown eyes, **bella** as can be,
The family was complete with the number three.

Giuseppa enjoyed playing with her friends from school,
In summer, they liked to go to the sea to stay cool.

She was growing up, as the years went by,
Soon she was dating and Tommaso started to cry.

Vincenzo came to sweep Giuseppa off her feet.
He brought her flowers and special treats.

Tommaso with his many jobs brought in the cash,
That was needed to pay for Giuseppa's big bash.

Giuseppa and Vincenzo were married by the light of the
moon.
Family and guests cheered with the rattling of the kitchen
spoons.

What was next for this young couple sitting next to the
palm tree?

They wanted to enjoy life, but they had to work and had responsibilities.

Giuseppa and Vincenzo Wedding

Vincenzo became a **carabiniere,** he arrested those who stole
The streets were safe in Mazara with "Enzo" on patrol.

Giuseppa, the cook in the **cucina**
She was always holding her **mappina.**

Vincenzo working the land,
Who always could use an extra hand.

Taking care of the house and all the chores,
They hardly found time to sit and relax outdoors.

There was a carnival every year.
The family celebrated and gave a cheer.

The sad **oggi** came when there was a knock at the door.
The news brought the family some hardship once more.

Tommaso could not believe it to be true,
But his dad, Gaspare, died and he felt very blue.

Gaspare was a smoker and his lungs were black.
He always wished that had given it up and never went back.

The family had gathered in Marsala to say their goodbyes
to a brave man.
It was an emotional day and hard to withstand.

Tommaso believed Gaspare was in a better place,
And watching over his family in Sicily and in the United
States.

Life was different now without his dad.
Sometimes it made him very sad.

But as time flew,
The family tree grew.

CHAPTER 4

Giuseppa and Her Wonderful News

Tommaso and Maria always wanted to become **Nonni,**
Giuseppa and her parents were enjoying gelato, the flavor
was spumoni.

Then she surprised her mom and dad.
A baby is on its way, and it made them very glad.

First Francesca was born in July of 1989.
The proud parents were thrilled, the baby was fine.

Francesca loved to help her mom and **nonna.**
And one day she would grow up like them, bella **donna.**

Another Carnival, more trips to the sea,
The family enjoyed playing cards, sometimes until three.

It's **Domenica,** whats for **pranzo**, or for **cena**? Wait and
find out.
Giuseppe and Maria are cooking; it will be amazing without
a doubt.

As Giuseppa started to feel not so great,
She went to the doctor who said it must be fate.

You are having baby number two,
Everyone was thrilled they didn't know what to do.

The 11th day of March was the day.
Marialuisa was born and she was ready to play.

Marialuisa as a young child so caring and sweet,
She had a laugh that if you heard it, you were in for a treat.

The sisters adored each other and always gave each other
a hug.
One day they hugged so much they almost tripped on their
rug.

The Town of Petrosino, where they live, was a lot of fun,
However, there was always work that had to be done.

The grapes needed picking and it was that time,
So the family harvested them off the vine.

Then the olives, so many to pick,
Green, black, small and big, they were all stuck on their stick.

When the harvest was complete,
Then it was time for a treat.

Let's have a party and dance all night.
Drink **vino** and **mangia** and try not to fight.

This family was very close at heart,
Nothing was going to change them and tear them apart.

**Giuseppa and her family
Francesca, Vincenzo, Giuseppa, and Marialuisa
photo 2015**

CHAPTER 5

The American Family:
Starting a New Life in New York

On that sad day at the New York pier,
What was to come would be clear.

Two brothers torn apart in front of their mother's eyes,
Their hearts broken, barely time to say their goodbyes.

Coming to America through Ellis Island and Brooklyn bound
Tears flowed from a crying mother, her husband and the
rest the family who were safe and sound.

Needing money and a place to stay,
Their sponsor helped them get through the day.

Praying for their son, Gaspare, and hoping he was not
too thin,
Took a lot out of them and it was hard for them to begin.

Carlo was the eldest son in America who had a heart of gold.
The brothers had a special bond, so they were told.

More children besides Carlo were born in New York,
Four girls and two boys fell out of the stork.

The family tree was growing larger and larger and had
more bills.
So the children left school, and went to work even if they
had the chills.

Twenty years plus had gone by and it was 1942.
Carlo worked a lot and he knew what he had to do.

Each job he spent a lot of time,
Working hard and trying to make more than a dime.

The company, Cascade, was a laundry business where he worked all day through.
Who knew that a Sicilian woman named Frances would work there too?

They enjoyed laughing and going out on dates,
Soon the wedding bells came and they became soul mates.

(Frances and Carlo Wedding Picture on Right)

Carlo and Frances had two girls, two years apart,
Anna and Fran were special sisters right from the start.

They loved their family and enjoyed their simple life.
The girls went to school, enjoyed their friends and ate Sunday dinner at Nonnis house without strife.

They were taught the American way,
And grew up in Brooklyn near the bay.

It was a struggle to put clothes on their back and food on
the plate,
But they worked hard and believed in fate.

The family decided the time was right,
To move to the country, and leave the city lights.

Anna, the eldest daughter graduated college then worked
in a NYC building so tall.
She married Albert, bought a house and had a baby, Greg,
who loved to crawl.

Frances, Carlo Anna and Fran

Grandpa Tommaso with Granddaughters, Fran and Anna

CHAPTER 6

Fran Follows her Dream!

Fran was a post college graduate who was voted the friendliest in her high school class of 1963.
She married Louis, had two children, a house and vacationed near the sea.

Fran was a Special Education Teacher in a tough neighborhood.
Carlo always encouraged her to read books, stay in school and she knew she would.

Carlo always told Fran he wondered where his brother Gaspare could be.
Was he even still in Sicily?

Did he marry or have a special friend?
He would be his brother until the end.

He always said before he died,
He would like to know about his brother in Sicily and then he cried.

Carlo and sister Lily told the family that it was unfair to say the least,
That Gaspare was in Sicily, and could never be here for the family feast.

The same year that Gaspare died, the bad news came,
Carlo was diagnosed with cancer and no one was to blame.

The doctors said a few months was all that he had,
Frances and the girls wanted to hug him every day and tried not to be sad.

His last breath came and all the family was there around seven.
He would be with his brother again very shortly in heaven.

Frances missed her husband Carlo, who was so dear,
She was lucky to have loved him for so many years.

Frances, Fran, Louis, Carlo

The American family tree is growing once more,
Fran and Louis had a daughter who liked to go with her
mom to the store.

Seven years later Carl was born and smiled every day.
He was a good baby who liked to sleep his day away.

Over the years, working and raising a family was her fate.
Fran knew that the family needed her and would never
hesitate.

When she turned fifty, her family came to a huge party to
celebrate.
It was a surprise that was pulled off just before eight.

Fun for Fran was her new logo.
Everyone knew that she would always be on the go.

Where is Fran, where could she be?
I think she just flew to Taipei on flight 753.

Her love for travel, family, and a good time,
Allowed her to get through each and every day, even when
her back was not fine.

She loves to read sitting in her favorite chair.
Her cats Oreo and Babycat, sit by her feet, they don't care.

Her life is fulfilled each and every day.
A truly special person, loved in every way.

CHAPTER 7

Jackie: The Energy Never Dies

Jackie was smart and enjoyed school.
She liked music, dance, sports and swimming in the pool.

She was like a general, since she was a kid.
She liked to boss around her friends and that's what she did.

A vacation to Disney, or while on a family camping trip,
Whichever it may be, you could count on Jackie to take a flip.

One day the skateboard went too fast and she took a wrong turn,
It wasn't her proudest moment, but definitely a lesson learned.

Her college years were filled with fun,
She barely managed to get her school work done.

Growing up in her twenties, a challenge to most,
She earned two masters degrees, but she doesn't like to boast.

It was tax day in April of 1999,
Jackie had an interview for a job and did just fine.

She always wanted to meet Mr. Right.
She found out during that interview it was love at first sight.

Ira came into her life, and he was sweet.
His love swept Jackie off her feet.

Carl, Louis, Fran, Jackie and Ira

First the wedding, the reception and the cake,
Would Jackie be a good wife and be able to bake?

Brownies, cookies, were just to name a few,
But there was something else in the oven and it grew!

September was the ninth month and Jackie was due.
The couple had a healthy baby boy who they could love too.

Jonathan was his name and his hair was auburn red.
He had beautiful blue eyes that sparkled as he awoke from his bed.

First nursery school, then elementary and now in junior high,
Boy, oh boy, doesn't time fly?

As a young child, Jonathan has shown,
He has become an expert at texting, and playing games on his phone.

Playing sports and his trumpet are a few ways that he has fun.
He also likes to compete on track and boy can he run.

Fran was now a grandma and happy to see the family tree grow.
She knew that she could retire and let teaching go.

Life was tough, but good for both families even though they were apart.

American or Italian, their family values always were close to the heart.

Jackie, Ira and Jonathan

CHAPTER 8

The Reunion across the Sea

As time went by the family tree was growing.
Technology, the internet, cell phones were flowing.

In 2013, an American couple was talking by a windowsill.
"Let's go this year to Italy", said Annie to her husband Bill.

Annie (Gaspare's niece) and Bill traveled to Sicily one day.
They had hoped to find their family that May.

The Albatros (B&B) was the place they stayed,
Where the breakfast was good and the beds were made.

Annie was determined and wanted to fulfill,
Her mom, Lily, and Uncle Carlos's dream to find their
family in Sicily with the assistance of Bill.

Looking through a phone book for the family name,
It was a long shot, but it was a part of the ancestry game.

When the phone rang, a nice fellow, Tommaso was on the
line.
Annie knew in her heart, her search was over and it was
barely nine.

Tommaso and Maria spoke a few minutes you see,
They needed a translator, Roberto, from the B and B.

It was a nice visit with Annie and Bill,
Both families could not have imagined the thrill.

A year went by and then it was the month of May.
Anita, Fran and Annie all three cousins came to visit from
the USA.

They had a special reunion with Tommaso, Maria and the gang.
There was so much laughing, it was hard to hear when the telephone rang.

The family had come together once again.
It was an amazing journey through time and they didn't want it to end.

Knock, knock, the neighbors came to the door to say "hi".
They wanted to meet the American cousins, before they said good bye.

**The Three American Cousins
(Anita, Annie and Fran)
Meet their Sicilian Cousin
Tommaso for the first time)**

The American cousins invited the Sicilian cousins to come
to New York and see USA places.
Their dream of their lifetime, you could see it on their faces.

It had to be discussed first with their mom and dad,
But Marialuisa and Francesca could not pass up this
opportunity, they were so glad.

So the planning of this trip in summer of 2014 came very
soon,
Everything was planned by the end of June.

CHAPTER 9

The Sicilian Dream to Come to America

The Sicilian Dream to come to America is a true story not a tale.
It starts with a girl name Marialuisa, who had an email.

She had found her American family one day.
It was when her cousins came from New York in that month of May.

She cried, she laughed, the whole day through.
She could not believe it to be true.

She was wearing her favorite color blue.
She started to translate until the trip was through.

Her friends, families and neighbors came from afar,
They brought espresso, cannolis, pasta and never sauce from a jar.

Marialuisa and Francesca sometimes were sad.
Soon their dreams would come true and they were very glad.

They wanted to travel to New York their entire life.
They wanted to do that before they became somebody's wife.

The trip was very long.
The girls remained strong.

Once they landed, upstate New York they went, it was about ten.
They visited their Cousin Annie's family; saw the countryside, the farms, and even a hen.

Sesame cookies were made and eaten.
Marialuisa and Francesca said the recipe could never be beaten.

They came to Long Island at last.
They had no idea they were about to have a blast!

More cousins, oh my, it really can't be.
Jackie and Fran said, "Yes, you have about 103"!

"I want to go to the beach," Marialuisa said,
Francesca wanted to swim in the pool instead.

The waves were too big not as common as they thought.
The girls knew another wave would come and they fought.

Let's remember the fun times at Splish Splash, the aquarium
and the birds that flew on our head,
The girls were so tired; they wanted to go to bed.

We laughed with all the fun adventures we had, but then
unfortunately we cried.
It was August 8, 2014 and Jackie's dad had unexpectedly
died.

The American Navy funeral for Louis, a tribute like no other,
The girls from Sicily completely understood and hugged
one another.

Witnessing the American flag folded so fine,
The cemetery was emotional and a very hard time.

Life was lonely without Jackie's dad,
The Sicilian cousins tried to cheer Jackie up and she was
glad.

New York City was on the list of places to see.
Can we go to Central Park and see all the birds in the trees?

Wait not a bird, a dog named BALTO or maybe a lake
named Jackie,
Could there be anything as wacky?

Times Square, the museum, the firemen, the buildings were so tall.
The girls loved them all and had a ball!

Marialuisa in Times Square - NYC

Enjoying Long Island where there is so much to do,
Here are some of the activities to name a few.

At Southaven Park, we all went on a rowboat.
It was a beautiful August day; we did not need a coat

The lake was calm
It had a lot of charm.

Heritage Park had grassy hills.
We ran up and down trying not to take a spill.

Islip is the town where you will find.
The Long Island Ducks Baseball team, they are one of a kind.

The Ducks are up and just like that, the baseball is hit hard and there goes the bat.

Jackie, Jonathan, Quackerjack, Marialuisa and Francesca L. I. Ducks Baseball

Remember the candy and snacks, there were a lot.
It was hard to get us out of the Port Jefferson or Uncle Giuseppe's parking lot.

We shopped at the stores, mall, outlets and more.
We tried not to spend too much money or we would not be able to shut the airplane door.

We planned a road trip to the American Capital, Washington D. C.
Maybe, President Obama could meet us for lunch near the great lawn tree?

The road trip would take a few days driving down South.
We packed the car and tried not to spill coffee out of our mouth.

There were seven of us that got in the blue van that day.
We could not believe it was 5AM and we were on our way.

First, there was New Jersey, then Delaware,
So many bridges to cross, they were everywhere.

Once we got to the Capital, there was so much to see.
We were starving, and ate at the McDonald's in D.C.

We took pictures, quite a few,
of the capital building, and the monuments too.

The air and space museum had rockets, planes and rocks
from outer space.
We enjoyed it but couldn't wait to go outside and eat ice
cream with the sun on our face.

Everyone, back in the car,
The timeshare is waiting, it's still far.

Virginia, here we come.
The fun has just begun!

Busch Gardens, an amusement park, the roller coasters,
are so high,
There are countries from Europe, no need to fly.

Animal shows and water flumes in Pompei,
All of us didn't want to leave, but wanted to stay.

Fireworks were firing high in the sky,
To patriotic music that made us cry.

The jacuzzi and resort were the top of the line.
We played games and laughed all night long and slept
until almost nine.

It rained in Williamsburg but we managed to go for a walk.
We ate and shopped and would always talk.

We talked about everything you could see,
Even a town named Petrosino which means Parsley.

Then there were the drinks to be had,
Soda, espresso, and wine that made us glad.

One morning, we had pancakes with chocolate chips
They were so good we did flips.

The blue van was packed; it was time to return to the beaches and the sun.
New York, watch out, these Sicilian girls plan to have fun!

The nicknames, we gave each other were so funny and true,
Giggles (Marialuisa), Muscles (Francesca), Movie Star (Fran) and the General (Jackie) are just to name a few.

Giggles and Muscles move to New York? What should they do?
Whatever is decided, we will always be cousins, friends and don't forget America loves you.

The trip to America was coming to an end.
The girls loved this country so much and will miss their new friends.

The question was asked, when will you come to Sicily and stay?
We replied perhaps in 2015, in the month of **Maggio,** May?

**General, Movie Star, Giggles and Muscles
Carlo's Italian Restaurant**

CHAPTER 10

The General and the Movie Star Arrive in Sicily!

Salina in Marsala

The year 2015 is finally here.
All the planning of the trip to Italy is getting near.

Daughter and mom ready to fly,
June 3 is the date, come say goodbye.

Our flight was to take off at three.
The General and Movie Star were excited as could be.

Up we go and we are in the air,
Six hours to go and we don't care.

Landing in Palermo, what should we do?
Rent a car or take a taxi or two?

The Fiat was finally ready for Jackie to drive
It was a white automatic that seated five.

Off Jackie and Fran went, driving very fast.
The roads were narrow and confusing but we had a blast.

"Meet us at the Hotel Baglio Basile parking lot," the Sicilian
cousins said.
"Do you see it?" "No, all we see is the traffic circle with a
flowerbed."

The family was standing in the street,
Jumping up and down and almost tripped on their feet.

Hugs and kisses were given to all.
The trip just started and we were going to have a ball.

Marialuisa and Francesca were in charge, not Jackie or Fran.
The plan was to see their favorite parts of Sicily, starting
with the sea and the sand.

The beauty of the Mediterranean Sea
What lies beyond is a mystery.

The cousins opened their house door.
We enjoyed the welcome and couldn't wait to see more.

At their house, Charlie their **cane**, played with his new toy.
Their **gatti** were purring and being good boys.

After a long journey and many miles that day, it was time to settle in.
Relaxing at the Bed and Breakfast, Albatros , was about to begin.

Strasatti market was the first stop, in the morning.
We ate **panelle**, bought a pocketbook, it was not boring.

Off to Petrosino Beach, that was near,
We went in the water it was so clear.

At the beach, we said, RUN, RUN RUN,
So we ran and jumped in the water and had some fun.

To Nonna Maria's **Casa** we went, her **cucina** smelled so nice
The couscous, manicotti, veal, and rabbit were perfect, no need for rice.

The cooking in Sicily is truly an art.
Olives, oranges, pasta, pastries, rice balls just to start.

We planned to leave for Palermo, the capital, at **sei,** 6 o' clock.

Family and friends would go in a van driven by Nino who lives around the block.

We would see Monreale, Mondello, the ships and find a nice place to eat.
A **bella** city experience, as we ate in a restaurant on the corner of the street.

Sunday morning is upon us.
We will visit **Saline**, we don't need a bus.

"The white Fiat will get us there," the girls said
"Hurry up; we have to take a boat instead."

The family is waiting for us to eat lunch at one.
"Tranquilla," the girls said, "We are not done."

The boat ride was beautiful, the islands too.
On the boat, we listened to the guide who told us what to do.

We got in the **macchina** after we paid the bill.
But the white Fiat could not get up the hill.

Muscles said with a strong voice, "**Andiamo!**"
We need to go to restaurant and, "**Mangiamo!**"

The family had lunch, the time was set
Now they are getting annoyed, I bet.

The buffet at the restaurant Baglio Basile, had pasta, chicken, meat and fish.
Each one of us spent some time filling our dish.

There was a lot of music and folk dancing at this fancy place.

We finished the afternoon with gelato and pastries on our face.

Petrosino – Hotel Baglio Basile – June 2015

Fran said, "Let's relax at the bed and breakfast, also called the B and B.
"Ok", said the girls, but tonight we go to Mazara del Vallo to eat pizza by the sea.

This pizza was topped with fresh vegetables, meat, sauce and cheese.
Everything so tasty and fresh, can we have more PLEASE!

Let's walk on the path and look at the sand.
Mazara is so picturesque; I think I hear a band.

Next, we are off to find a place to eat Gelato, in a cone or a cup.
It was late and we could barely stand up.

Monday was the last day of our stay.
We will come back again one day.

Tommaso and the girls came to the bed and breakfast to see,
On the table were the most delicious pastries and espresso coffee.

Fruit, chocolate or custard, inside the puff,
It was so tasty with all that stuff.

Last stop, the barbeque, the meat and veggies were on the grill.
Maria and Giuseppa are amazing cooks and never sat still.

Gianluca, Romina, Elisa, and Margherita are friends and neighbors that are coming to stay,
We brought plenty of American fun games for them to play.

Jump rope, Frisbee, and chalk to name a few,
We were running out of time, there was so much to do.

We said our goodbyes to Petrosino and hope to see you soon,
Everyone wished their American family well, and hoped to see us next, **Giugno**, June.

CHAPTER 11

Mainland Italy- Rome and the Amalfi Coast

"I bought the tickets," the General said, "We are good to go to Rome."
The girls couldn't believe it; they were so surprised and yelled around their home.

Our trip included four days in Rome,
There is where we experienced a big beautiful dome.

When in Rome you will find,
a truly remarkable city with people who are kind.

Eating out or ordering in,
The food in Rome is so good you don't even know where
to begin.

The girls said, "It's Wednesday and Pope Francis is at his
house."We need to leave before nine."
Let's get tickets, hurry up and get in line.

Even though it was hot,
We waited in line a lot.

Seeing the Pope was a
dream that could not be
beat.
It was worth every minute
of our tiring feet.

Vatican City is an amazing place to see,
One of the most popular tourists sites in the country.

There were two floors on a pink bus.
It stopped at the city sights, to show all of us.

The Mouth of Truth was so big and round.
We put our hands in and hoped it didn't bite down.

The days in Sorrento were at a B and B.
The boats were amazing down by the sea.

What happened next was a memory that will never fade.
We took a boat ride to Capri and were never in the shade.

There were ten tourists and one captain aboard.
The waves got rough and bumpy we tried not to fall overboard.

Seeing a waterfall and jumping in to swim with the fish,
But wait, our lunch is waiting on the isle of Capri in the dish.

Laughing all the way back and trying not to get wet,
The cousins were lying on the back of the boat and they were set.

The lemons smelled so good and the **giallo** color shined so.
Sorrento had the best Limoncello!

The trip was getting better every day,
especially with a private car and driver, Antonino, leading us all the way.

Driving the Amalfi coast looking at the sea,
There is no other place I would rather be.

The trip was slowly coming to an end.
The airport was just around the bend.

We visited Pompeii, an ancient town from the past,
an experience through time which would always last.

The Volcano at Vesuvius so big and rough,
Looking up at you, you don't seem that tough.

As we started the mighty climb to the top of the crater,
We had to hurry before the gates closed and would lock
us in there later.

It was close but we came out at five.
The movie star was still shopping and didn't even know if
we made it out alive.

Eating Pizza in the hotel room and laughing all night,
We didn't know if we were going to catch our morning flight.
Naples airport was nearby.
We knew we were all about to cry.

The Movie Star and General headed back to USA,
Muscles and Giggles, their next stop was Palermo that
same day.

The Amalfi Coast and Sorrento

The Lost Branch Together Forever!

So long ago, a child (the lost branch) taken away from its tree,
A family united, thanks to research and ancestry.

The story continues after the closing of the airplane door.
It was decided a book was to be made which will include
all four.

The lost branch found, no longer apart from its tree,
to grow together and forget the past and live in harmony.

The future has not yet been told; so let us believe in fate.
The adventures and memories will come, when we meet
again so let us never hesitate.

Special cousins across the seas,
They would be together once again, American and Sicilian
families.

Two distant lands but united by fate,
We love both countries Italy and the United States.

A Letter Written to Grandma in Italy from her Grandson during his voyage to America

Dear Grandma,

I am on the ship to America and the food is horrible. The reason I left is because Mom is sad and Dad lost his job, also the taxes are way too high. I am with them now and we all hope for a better life in America. When we left we knew of many people whose crops were dying and could not make money.

There is a big storm coming. I am starting to get sea sick and my bunk is as hard as a rock. The worst part is that there are no sheets so I freeze at night. We went steerage because we had $23. We did not get first class because you had to have more money. The captain has said only three more days until we get to America. That has been the only exciting news for now. We are hoping to get passed this storm but I really want to get through Ellis Island so I can start our new life in America. I hope to not have to go back like some people.

Now we are getting off the boat. I see the Statue of Liberty. It is 305 feet tall. I am about to get checked. Dad, mom and Maria passed all the medical checks and so did I but not Gaspare. He has to return to Sicily. All of us are extremely upset and do not want him to go but they insist because of an eye problem. Dad has to get a job and mom is crying all the time. We will find a place to live which will be small since it will be all that we can afford. I am really happy to live in America but I wish my brother was here with us. Don't know when we will ever be together as a family again.

Love,
Carlo Titone (10 years old)

Glossary for bold words in story with Italian to English translation

Bella- beautiful
Carabiniere - policeman
Cucina- kitchen
Mappina- kitchen dish towel
Oggi- today
Nonna- grandma
Nonno – grandpa
Nonni - grandparents
Donna - woman
Domenica- Sunday
Pranzo- lunch
Cena- dinner
Tranquilla- relax
Ragazza- girl
Vino- wine
Mangia- eat
Cane- dog
Gatti- cats
Panelle – street fair food made with chick peas
Saline- salt mill

Macchina - car
Giallo- yellow
Andiamo – hurry up
Mangiamo – lets all eat

Learn to count to ten in Italian

1 - uno
2 - due
3 - tre
4 - quattro
5 - cinque
6 - sei
7 - sette
8 - otto
9 - nove
10 – dieci

Days of the Week

Sunday - Domenica
Monday- Lunedì
Tuesday- Martedì
Wednesday- Mercoledì
Thursday- Giovedì
Friday- Venerdì
Saturday- Sabato

Months of the Year

January- Gennaio

February-Febbraio
March- Marzo
April- Aprile
May- Maggio
June- Giugno
July- Luglio
August- Agosto
September- Settembre
October- Ottobre
November- Novembre
December- Dicembre

Italian Survival Words

Vorrei – I would like
Devo – I have to
Posso – I can
Mi piace – I like
Vedo che – I see that
Ho bisogno di – I need
Mi porti – Bring me
Mi mostri – Show me
Ha lei? – Do you have…?
E' possiblile? - Is it possible?
Mi mandi – Send me
Mi dia – Give me
Mi dica – Tell me
Non voglio – I don't want
Dove sono…? - Where are…?
Dove? – Where?

Come? – How?

Quando? – When?

Perche? Why? Because!

A che ora? – At what time?

Quale? – Which one?

Come si dice? – How do you say?

Ho, non ho – I have, I don't have

Questo – This

Ecco – Here is

Chi e? – Who is it?

Quello – That one

Quanto? – How much?

Desidero – I want

Qui – here

Sono stanco/a – I'm tired

Per piacere – please

Grazie – thank you

Ciao, Buon giorno – Hello, good day

Buono sera – good evening

Che, Che cosa, cosa? - what?

Sono – they are

Ho fame – I'm hungry

Ho sete – I'm thirsty

Ho freddo – I'm cold

Ho caldo – I'm hot

Characters in the Story from Sicily

Tommaso (deceased) – Born in 1877 - father of Gaspare, Carlo, Mary, Carmella (Lily), Twin Girls (who died very young), Philip and Michael. He came to New York to begin a new life with his wife Anna, two eldest sons, and daughter. The other children were born in America.

Anna- (deceased) wife of Tommaso and mother to eight children listed above. She suffered many times in her life including: when her oldest son was taken from her arms at Ellis Island and sent back to Sicily. Then her twin girls died when they were two years old of pneumonia.

Gaspare- (deceased) oldest son who had to return to his homeland without his family to live with Aunt and Uncle, he had a special bond with his brother Carlo.

Carlo- (deceased)brother of Gaspare, who was upset when his brother was taken by immigration police, lived in America with Mary, Lily, Philip and Michael, wife Frances, Father of Anna and Frances , Grandfather to Jackie, "the general", Carl and Gregory.

Giuseppa-(deceased) married Gaspare – mother to Tommaso, two boys and two girls.

Tommaso - oldest son of Gaspare and Giuseppa- Father of Giuseppa, husband to Maria, Grandfather to Francesca and Marialuisa, First Cousin to Annie, Fran and Anita, Anna

Maria- Tommaso lovely wife, mother of Giuseppa and grandmother of Francesca and Marialuisa

Giuseppa- daughter of Tommaso and Maria and wife of Vincenzo, mother of Francesca and Marialuisa

Vincenzo- husband of Giuseppa, recently retired from being a police officer in Mazara De Vallo

Francesca – daughter of Giuseppa and Vincenzo- also known as Muscles in book

Marialuisa- daughter of Giuseppa and Vincenzo- also known as Giggles in book

Roberto and Paolo - two brothers who assisted in translation during the initial reunion– The Meo Family – the owners of the Bed and Breakfast Albratros located in Marsala

Gianluca, Romina, Elisa- Close friends and neighbors across the street from Marialuisa and Francesca

Margherita- a special friend of family who dances into everyone's hearts.

Characters in the Story from America

Annie – granddaughter of Tommaso, daughter of Carmella (Lily), first cousin to Tommaso, Fran, Annie

Bill- husband to Annie who took initial reunion trip to find family in Sicily

Anita – first cousin to Tommaso, Fran, Annie, took reunion trip in 2013 to meet the Sicilian Cousins

Frances-(deceased) wife of Carlo, mother of Anna and Fran, Grandmother to Jackie, Carl, and Gregory

Anna- granddaughter of Tommaso and Anna, eldest daughter of Carlo and Frances- wife of Albert, mother of Gregory

Albert- husband of Anna, father of Gregory

Gregory- son of Anna and Albert, grandson of Carlo and Frances

Fran- granddaughter of Tommaso and Anna youngest daughter of Carlo and Frances, wife of Louis, mother to Jackie and Carl

Louis- (deceased) husband to Frances and father to Jackie and Carl

Carl- great grandson to Tommaso and Anna, grandson to Carlo and Frances, second child of Fran and Louis and brother to Jackie

Jackie- great granddaughter to Tommaso and Anna, granddaughter to Carlo and Frances, first child of Fran and Louis and sister to Carl

Ira- husband to Jackie and father of Jonathan

Jonathan- great great grandson to Tommaso and Anna and great grandson to Carlo and Frances, grandson to Fran and Louis, son of Jackie and Ira

<u>Lessons to be learned from both near and far:</u>
Don't Worry Be Happy!
Non preoccuparti sii felice!

Don't let you dreams stay dreams, they are never too far
Believe in yourself and stay true to who you are

If you believe
You will achieve

Believe in fate,
Don't hesitate

Work and play
Have fun everyday

Giggles, Muscles, the Movie Star and General will show
you the way!

Biography of Fran (editor), "The Movie Star"

Fran is 71 years old and lives in Coram, New York. She is a retired Special Education Teacher and College Professor. She has two children, one grandson, three cats and three grand dogs. She enjoys reading, spending time with friends, and traveling the world.

Biography of Jackie (author), "The General"

Jackie is 46 years old and resides in Long Island, New York. She is a full time Clinical Exercise Physiologist in Cardiac Rehabilitation for the past 20 years. She is married and has one son. Her interests include hiking, skiing, playing piano, tennis, and walking her dog Woody. She loves to travel when time allows.

Biography of Francesca (coordinator of photos), "Muscles"

Francesca is 27 years old. She lives in Petrosino, Sicily. She is a very diligent and hard worker since she was 16 years old. Her work includes hotel service, customer service for a utility company and salesperson in the clothing industry. Her passion is for social work. She has volunteered in organizations which provide services for the less fortunate. She loves her family, her pets and loves to travel.

Biography of Marialuisa (illustrator) "Giggles"

Marialuisa is 21 years old. She lives in Petrosino, Sicily. She graduated in the top two percent of her High School, Geometra. Her expertise in English earned her a trip of a lifetime to study in England. With her passion for learning and her interests of photography, illustrating, and music, she will one day find her dream career. She loves spending time with her family, friends and enjoys all animals. Traveling and visiting the United States has always been her dream.

The story of my Sicilian connection is fun to tell. I hope you enjoy learning a little bit about Sicily, and how our family in America reconnected with our relatives across the sea. There were two brothers that were separated at a young age because of the strict rules of immigration back in the early 1900's. A hundred years later, a reunion of two families finally took place. There were sad times, happy adventures and special moments and memories that will last a lifetime.

CPSIA information can be obtained
at www.ICGtesting.com
Printed in the USA
BVOW05s1542190817
492355BV00009B/5/P